ARTIFICIAL INTELLIGENCE
The Silent Revolution That Transforms the World and Your Income

Table of Contents

Chapter 1: Artificial Intelligence: A Concept Within Everyone's Reach
1.1 What is Artificial Intelligence?
• 1.1.1 Simple definition and everyday applications
• 1.1.2 The history of AI: from early experiments to the present day
1.2 The Philosophy Behind AI: A New Way of Thinking
• 1.2.1 From rational thinking to algorithmic thinking
• 1.2.2 How ancient philosophers would have interpreted AI
1.3 Competitors in the Market: The Impact of Amazon and Its Income Potential
• 1.3.1 AI Innovation in Commerce
• 1.3.2 Earning Potential

Chapter 2: AI and Your Business: How to Get Started Without Being an Expert
2.1 Easy-to-Use AI Tools
• 2.1.1 Artificial intelligence platforms accessible to everyone
• 2.1.2 How to start with applications for small businesses
2.2 Automation of Repetitive Tasks
• 2.2.1 Saving time and optimizing communication with chatbots
• 2.2.2 Email and Social Media Management Tools
2.3 Earning in Small Steps: Monetizing AI
• 2.3.1 Creating Engaging Content with AI for Your Blog or YouTube Channel
• 2.3.2 Earning opportunities with dropshipping and AI

Chapter 3: AI and Marketing: Reaching Your Audience
3.1 Understanding Customer Data with AI
• 3.1.1 How AI analyzes consumer behavior

- 3.1.2 Using insights to improve sales

3.2 Personalized Marketing Strategies
- 3.2.1 Creating targeted advertising campaigns
- 3.2.2 Practical examples of personalization with AI

3.3 Competitors in Digital Marketing: Google and Its Solutions
- 3.3.1 Google's automated marketing tools
- 3.3.2 Case study: Companies that have benefited from Google's AI

Chapter 4: Creativity Enhanced by AI

4.1 Generating Creative Content
- 4.1.1 Writing articles and stories with AI
- 4.1.2 Creating art and design with AI tools

4.2 Music and Video: AI as a Collaborator
- 4.2.1 Composing songs with AI
- 4.2.2 Automatically Editing Videos: How to Do It

4.3 AI in Media Production
- 4.3.1 Examples of companies using AI in media
- 4.3.2 How creators are leveraging AI

Chapter 5: AI for Personal and Professional Improvement

5.1 AI-Based Learning Tools
- 5.1.1 Educational Platforms Utilizing AI
- 5.1.2 How AI personalizes the learning experience

5.2 Skill Development with AI
- 5.2.1 Continuous training through intelligent tools

5.3 Philosophy and Personal Growth: AI as a Guide
- 5.3.1 AI for Improving Daily Life
- 5.3.2 AI as a tool for self-discovery and improvement

Chapter 6: AI in the Financial Sector: Earning Intelligently

6.1 Financial Data Analysis with AI
- 6.1.1 How AI can help make better investments
- 6.1.2 User-Friendly Financial Analysis Tools

6.2 Automation of Personal Finances
- 6.2.1 Apps that manage daily expenses
- 6.2.2 Optimizing savings and investments with AI

6.3 Competitors in the Sector: Robinhood and Investment Accessibility
- 6.3.1 How Robinhood has changed the way people invest
- 6.3.2 Democratized Investment Opportunities with AI

Chapter 7: The Future of AI: Opportunities and Challenges

7.1 Future Perspectives for Artificial Intelligence
- 7.1.1 Emerging sectors where AI will have a significant impact
- 7.1.2 Preparing for a Future Dominated by AI

7.2 Ethics and Responsibility in AI Use
- 7.2.1 Philosophical reflections on ethics and technology
- 7.2.2 The importance of responsibility in AI adoption

7.3 Preparing for Imminent Changes
- 7.3.1 Required Skills in the Future Labor Market
- 7.3.2 How to remain competitive in an evolving world

Chapter 8: Earnings and the Transformation of the World

8.1 A Future to Govern with Awareness
- 8.1.1 The challenge of human change
- 8.1.2 Work and the disappearance of historical professions

8.2 Humanity in the Age of AI
- 8.2.1 Creativity, emotion, and human identity in the Age of AI
- 8.2.2 Delegating Decisions and the Risk of Alienation: Where Does Human Control Stop?

8.3 The Tax Regulation of AI Earnings

- 8.3.1 The dilemma of international taxation of AI
- 8.3.2 The risk of tax evasion

Chapter 9: The Legal Approach to AI: An Incomplete Framework
9.1 AI Regulation: An Evolving Framework
- 9.1.1 Ethical and legal dilemmas
- 9.1.2 A Future to Govern Wisely

Conclusions

Imagine a change that slips like a whisper into the fabric of reality, an imperceptible movement that transforms the way we perceive the world. It is not a visible alteration, not immediate nor loud, but profound and radical, like an underground current that moves the roots of our existence. We find ourselves on the edge of a metamorphosis that involves not only what we do, but the very essence of being.

There is an invisible force, capable of altering the boundary between what we once thought possible and what now appears inevitable. This force doesn't merely rewrite the rules of our daily lives; it raises ancient questions, prompting us to reconsider who we are and where we are headed. It almost feels as if the world is breathing a new thought, a new consciousness expanding beyond our control, challenging our limits, and unveiling dimensions yet unexplored.

This is not merely about progress or innovation. It is the beginning of a reflection that touches the deepest chords of human existence: the essence of thought, the nature of creation, the complexity of the intertwining between us and what we do not yet understand. This book is an invitation to explore these hidden horizons, to look beyond the visible, to be guided by the most radical questions that arise when the barriers of imagination and reality itself are shattered.

Chapter 1
Artificial Intelligence: A Concept Within Everyone's Reach

1.1 What is Artificial Intelligence?

1.1.1 Simple Definition and Everyday Applications

Artificial intelligence (AI) is a term we hear more and more often, but what does it really mean?
In simple terms, AI refers to technology that allows computers and programs to mimic human cognitive functions. Imagine having an assistant that can not only follow commands but also learn from your preferences, solve complex problems, and interact with you naturally. This is the goal of AI: to make machines "intelligent" so that they can assist us in everyday life.
AI relies on algorithms and learning models that enable computers to process large amounts of data, recognize patterns, and make predictions. There are several subcategories of AI, including:
Machine Learning: This is the process through which computers "learn" from data. For example, an AI system can analyze a customer's purchasing habits and use that information to suggest products that might interest them.
Natural Language Processing: This technology allows computers to understand and interact in human language. It's what enables chatbots to answer questions and voice assistants to execute voice commands.
Computer Vision: AI can also "see" and interpret images and videos. This is used in applications such as facial recognition and document scanning.
Today, AI is present in many areas of our daily lives, even if we often don't realize it. Here are some common applications:
Voice Assistants: Siri, Google Assistant, and Alexa are examples of virtual assistants that use AI to answer questions, manage reminders, and control

home devices. These assistants can understand and respond to voice commands, making it easier and quicker to access information.

Personalized Recommendations: When you watch a movie on Netflix or shop on Amazon, you probably notice that the system suggests content or products that might interest you. This is the result of AI algorithms analyzing your preferences and past behaviors.

Customer Service Chatbots: Many companies use AI-based chatbots to provide immediate support to customers. These bots can answer frequently asked questions, help with order issues, and even manage bookings, all without the need for a human operator.

Automatic Translation: Services like Google Translate use AI to translate texts and conversations in real time. This facilitates communication between people who speak different languages, making the world more connected.

Navigation and Maps: Applications like Google Maps and Waze use AI to analyze traffic in real time and provide optimal routes. These tools can also alert you to accidents or congestion, helping you save time during your commutes.

Fitness and Health: Many health-tracking apps, such as those used to count steps or monitor sleep, use AI to analyze data and provide personalized advice to improve well-being.

Artificial intelligence is not just a futuristic technology but is already an integral part of our daily lives. With applications ranging from voice assistants to personalized recommendations, AI is changing the way we interact with the world. It is accessible to everyone, regardless of technological expertise. In the following lines, we will explore in detail how AI can be used to improve our lives, simplify our daily activities, and ultimately pave the way for new opportunities for earning and innovation.

1.1.2 The History of AI: From Early Experiments to Today

Artificial intelligence (AI) has its roots in the 1940s and 1950s when Alan Turing proposed the concept of thinking machines. In 1956, the term "artificial intelligence" was coined during the Dartmouth Conference, marking the official beginning of AI research.

In the 1960s and 1970s, optimism grew with the development of board game programs and the first expert systems, but excessive expectations led to the first "AI winter" in the 1970s, with a slowdown in funding and development.

In the 1980s, interest in AI was revived with the emergence of neural networks and expert systems. With the arrival of machine learning in the 1990s and deep learning in 2010, AI experienced an explosion of practical applications, becoming an integral part of our daily lives, from online recommendations to virtual assistants. Today, AI is at the center of innovations that promise to further transform our future.

1.2 The Philosophy Behind AI: A New Way of Thinking

1.2.1 From Rational Thinking to Algorithmic Thinking

Artificial intelligence marks a fundamental shift in how we conceive of thinking and rationality. Traditionally, rational thinking has been seen as an intrinsically human ability, driven by logic, intuition, and emotions. Philosophers like Aristotle and Descartes emphasized the importance of reason and self-reflection in human decision-making.

With the emergence of AI, however, we are witnessing a shift toward "algorithmic thinking." Here, decisions and evaluations are based on mathematical and statistical models rather than personal experiences or rationality. This shift raises profound questions about the nature of intelligence itself: can an algorithm really "think"? And what are the ethical implications of delegating decision-making to machines? The philosophy of AI invites reflection on these questions, exploring how the interaction between humanity and technology can redefine our notions of intelligence and consciousness.

1.2.2 How Ancient Philosophers Would Interpret AI

Let's imagine bringing ancient philosophers, such as Plato, Aristotle, and Seneca, to our time to explore the phenomenon of artificial intelligence. For Plato, AI might appear as a reflection of the world of ideas, an attempt to reproduce the ideal of intelligence and rationality, but always imperfect compared to the true essence of human intellect.

Aristotle, on the other hand, might question the logic and ethics of AI. For him, the ability to reason is central to humanity; therefore, delegating decisions to a machine would raise moral dilemmas: can machines be responsible for their actions?

Seneca, with his Stoic vision, would see in AI an opportunity to improve human life but would warn of the risks of excessive dependence on technology. True wisdom, for him, would lie in finding a balance between the use of human reason and the assistance of machines.

In this light, artificial intelligence is not just a technological issue but a profound philosophical question that invites us to reflect on our very being, our rationality, and the values that guide our lives.

1.3 Competitors in the Market: The Impact of Amazon and Its Earning Potential

1.3.1 AI Innovation in Commerce

Many large e-commerce companies, such as Amazon, have invested heavily in artificial intelligence to optimize their logistics operations and improve the personalization of the user experience. Through the use of advanced algorithms, these companies can analyze customer data and offer personalized recommendations, increasing sales and enhancing customer loyalty. Amazon Web Services (AWS), the cloud computing division of the well-known U.S. e-commerce giant, also offers AI tools that enable other companies to leverage AI for their operations, thus amplifying Amazon's reach and influence in the market.

1.3.2 Earning Potential

Amazon's AI-related earning potential is immense. Through the automation of processes such as inventory management and logistics, Amazon reduces operational costs and improves efficiency. In addition, the expansion of AI services through AWS not only generates significant revenue but also creates new opportunities for businesses of all sizes. This strategic positioning allows Amazon not only to dominate the e-commerce market but also to become a key player in the AI ecosystem, offering scalable and innovative solutions for businesses worldwide. With the continued evolution of AI, Amazon is well-positioned to further capitalize on these technologies, consolidating its leadership in the sector.

Chapter 2
AI and Your Business: How to Start Without Being an Expert

Artificial intelligence (AI) may seem like a technology reserved for experts and large companies, but it actually offers opportunities accessible even to those running small businesses or just starting out. In this chapter, we will explore how to use AI to optimize your business without the need for advanced technical skills. We will look at easy-to-use tools, how to automate repetitive tasks, and strategies for monetizing AI.

2.1 Easy-to-Use AI Tools

2.1.1 Artificial Intelligence Platforms Accessible to Everyone

Today, there are numerous artificial intelligence platforms that make the use of these technologies accessible to everyone. Services like ChatGPT, Canva with AI, and Copy.ai offer user-friendly interfaces that allow even beginners to generate content, write texts, or create graphics with just a few clicks.

These platforms do not require programming skills and offer tutorials and step-by-step guides to help you get started. Experimenting with these tools allows you to become familiar with AI and understand how it can fit into your business needs. Whether you want to write social media posts or design marketing materials, AI is here to simplify your life.

ChatGPT is a powerful text generation tool that can help you write content quickly and effectively. Here's how to use it best:
Start with a Clear Question: When using ChatGPT, formulating a clear and specific question is essential. For example, instead of asking, "Tell me about marketing," try "What are the best marketing strategies for a small business?" This helps the model provide you with more relevant answers.
Experiment with Requests: Don't be afraid to try

different formulations to get the desired result. You can also ask ChatGPT to give you examples or practical suggestions, like "Give me five ideas for social media posts."
Review and Adapt: After getting a response, take the time to review the content. Add your personal touch or edit the parts that don't exactly reflect your style.

Canva has integrated artificial intelligence features that further simplify graphic design. Here's how to start:
Choose a Template: Canva offers a wide range of predefined templates for presentations, social media posts, flyers, and more. Choose a template that fits your project and start customizing it.
Use the "Magic Resize" Feature: This feature allows you to automatically resize your design to fit different formats (for example, from a Facebook post to an Instagram story) without having to start over from scratch.
Explore Text and Image Suggestions: With AI, Canva can suggest phrases or images based on the type of content you're creating. It's a great way to find inspiration if you're unsure where to start.

2.1.2 How to Start with Applications for Small Businesses

In an increasingly digital world, small businesses have the opportunity to thrive by adopting AI-based tools. These tools not only simplify business processes but also improve efficiency and increase profits, making them accessible even to those with less technical experience. Let's explore how to begin implementing AI applications to optimize business and capitalize on new opportunities.

How to Identify Areas for Improvement?
The first step in integrating AI into your small business is to critically assess your operations. It's crucial to understand where AI can bring significant improvements, such as reducing the time spent on

repetitive tasks or better addressing customer needs. Here are some questions to start this reflection:

- Which business processes take too much time and are repetitive? This could include social media management, responding to emails, or handling sales.
- Where are the bottlenecks? Identifying inefficiencies helps find effective solutions.
- How can you better meet customer needs with AI? Think about how AI tools can help you provide quick and personalized responses.

This analysis not only helps you outline intervention areas but also allows you to consider how your business can evolve to compete better in today's market. AI is not just a technical solution but a true growth strategy.

Selecting the Right AI Tools
Once you've identified the areas where AI can be helpful, it's time to choose the applications that meet your specific needs. For small businesses, there are many simple and intuitive platforms that offer advanced AI functionalities, such as:

- Smart CRMs: Customer relationship management systems that analyze data to improve interaction and retention.
- Chatbots: Virtual assistants that handle FAQs and assist customers 24/7, saving time and improving customer satisfaction.
- Marketing automation tools: Platforms like Mailchimp or HubSpot use AI to segment audiences, send automated emails, and analyze engagement data.

It's important not to immediately go for the most expensive or complex solution. Start small, testing free versions to see if the application fits your needs without risking a high initial investment. Here are some practical tips to get started:

- Test free versions: Before subscribing, take advantage of free versions of platforms to test their features.
- Identify key needs: If you run an e-commerce store, for example, Shopify offers AI tools for sales analysis and inventory management, while Hootsuite simplifies social media management.
- Automate gradually: Introduce AI step by step into your operations. Start with simple tasks like content scheduling and automated email sending.

Training and Gradual Adoption
AI implementation doesn't have to happen overnight, and adoption can involve a learning curve. If you don't have a dedicated IT team, investing in staff training is crucial. Not everyone is immediately ready to work with new technologies, but by providing the right resources and fostering an environment open to experimentation, you can ease the adoption process.

Some ideas on how to handle the transition:

- Internal training sessions: Organize workshops for your team, showing how to use new applications and encouraging collaboration.
- Tutorials and support: Provide step-by-step guides and tutorials that staff can follow to familiarize themselves with new tools.
- Open environment: Create a trusting atmosphere where every team member feels free to ask for help and share feedback.

Monitoring Results and Adapting Strategies
Finally, it's essential to regularly monitor the results from using AI applications. Use clear metrics to evaluate the effectiveness of your new strategies. These could include increased sales, reduced response time to customers, or improved overall customer satisfaction. Some practical suggestions:

- Assess the impact on sales: E-commerce platforms like Shopify provide detailed reports

on sales and product performance. Analyze this data to optimize your decisions.
- Measure engagement: Tools like Mailchimp allow you to monitor email marketing campaign metrics, such as open and click rates. Use this data to improve future campaigns.
- Adapt strategies: AI is constantly evolving, and so should your business strategies. Don't be afraid to make adjustments and optimize your applications as you gather new information.

Integrating AI may seem complex at first, but with a well-planned strategy and tools suited to your needs, small businesses can gain great benefits, optimizing processes, boosting sales, and opening new monetization opportunities.

2.2 Automating Repetitive Tasks

2.2.1 Saving Time and Optimizing Communication with Chatbots

Chatbots are one of the most effective solutions for improving efficiency and customer interaction by automating much of the repetitive communication. Services like ManyChat and Tidio not only simplify the management of frequently asked questions but also free up valuable time that you can dedicate to higher-value strategic activities. These tools transform how companies interact with their customers, offering quick and personalized responses that enhance the overall user experience.

A well-configured chatbot doesn't just respond to predefined questions but becomes a true virtual assistant, capable of gathering data, managing bookings, following up on orders, and even recommending products or services. This way, you not only optimize the handling of requests but also create a tailored experience for each customer, increasing engagement and trust in your brand.

To implement a chatbot successfully, it's essential to choose a platform that easily integrates with the tools you already use, like Facebook Messenger or your website. Configuration is often simple, thanks to numerous tutorials and user-friendly interfaces that allow you to customize responses in detail. Through careful definition of questions and answers, you can ensure that the bot provides accurate and relevant information while maintaining your brand's communication tone and style.

Automation via chatbots not only relieves the daily workload but also allows you to focus on what truly grows your business: innovation, expansion strategies, and developing new products or services. Instead of manually responding to the same questions, you can spend your time and that of your team on more creative and productive activities, bringing real added value to your company.

Additionally, chatbots provide valuable insights into customer interactions. You can track which questions are asked most frequently, identify common issues, and see which products generate the most interest, allowing you to continuously optimize both customer service and your commercial offerings. Adopting a chatbot is not just a step toward operational efficiency but a way to build a stronger, more personalized relationship with your customers, contributing to the long-term success of your business.

2.2.2 Email and Social Media Management Tools

Optimizing Time and Enhancing Strategies

In the ever-evolving digital world, managing emails and social media can easily become one of the most time-consuming tasks. However, AI offers advanced tools that not only simplify these tasks but transform them into highly efficient and strategic processes. Using platforms like Buffer and Zapier, for instance, doesn't just mean automating publishing but gaining a more refined control and overview of your digital campaigns.

Planning and Automating Social Media

Buffer is one of the most powerful tools for social media management, allowing you to schedule and publish your posts in advance, maintaining a constant presence without having to be always active on various channels. The real usefulness of Buffer lies in the ability to create a detailed content calendar, enabling you to plan weeks or months of posts with just a few clicks. This feature not only saves you valuable time but also allows you to monitor the performance of your publications, analyzing engagement and optimizing your strategy based on the collected data.

Automation here is not just a time-saver but an opportunity to maintain consistent and targeted communication with your audience. In an era where user attention is a rare commodity, consistency in messages and published content becomes crucial in creating a lasting and trustworthy bond with your followers. Additionally, Buffer offers the ability to analyze the performance of your posts, providing you with detailed data on audience interaction, allowing you to continuously refine your approach.

Automating Email Campaigns

As for email management, tools like Mailchimp offer a wide range of features that simplify campaigns, from onboarding new subscribers to sending periodic promotions or newsletters. One of Mailchimp's most effective features is the ability to set up automations based on specific behaviors or events, such as a new user registration or a product purchase. With just a few steps, you can create automated email sequences sent at the right time, increasing conversion rates and customer retention.

The effectiveness of these automations lies in their ability to personalize communication, maintaining an authentic and timely tone without requiring continuous intervention on your part. For example, you can create welcome emails for new subscribers, remind customers of an abandoned cart, or send targeted promotions based on each audience segment's specific interests. In this way, your communication is not only automated but also becomes strategic and focused on increasing engagement and sales opportunities.

Connecting Everything with Zapier: The Magic of Automation
Zapier, on the other hand, acts as a link between different platforms, allowing you to automate repetitive tasks and connect workflows smoothly. For example, you can create "zaps" that integrate your social media with your email campaigns, ensuring that every new newsletter subscription is automatically added to your contact list and that welcome or promotional emails are sent without manual intervention. You can also connect tools like Buffer to Google Sheets or Slack to track post performance in real-time or notify your team about completed tasks.

A Broad Strategic Vision
By combining these tools, you can holistically manage your digital communication, transforming tasks that would take hours into automated workflows that run in the background. What makes these solutions truly powerful is not just the automation of daily activities but the opportunity to continuously analyze, measure, and optimize your campaigns without compromising the quality of your customer contact.

Ultimately, maximizing email and social media management tools means not only saving time but also freeing up resources to focus on what truly matters: creating more impactful communication strategies, building meaningful relationships with your audience, and intelligently and sustainably growing your business.

2.3 Earning in Small Steps: Monetizing AI

2.3.1 Creating Engaging Content with AI for Your Blog or YouTube Channel

In an era where creativity and productivity seem to walk a fine line, artificial intelligence (AI) emerges as a valuable and powerful ally for those looking to stand out in the world of digital content. Advanced tools like Jasper and Lumen5 represent much more than simple platforms; they are true creative collaborators capable of revolutionizing the way we think and create content for blogs and YouTube channels.

These tools go beyond automated generation; they analyze search trends, audience preferences, and communication strategies to suggest relevant and engaging content. With Jasper, for example, you can generate high-quality articles in minutes, tailoring texts to your audience and adjusting the tone and style according to the message you want to convey. Lumen5, on the other hand, allows you to transform a simple article into an engaging video, using images, animations, and sounds that capture attention and keep audience interaction alive.

But it's not just about efficiency. These tools open the door to new creative possibilities: they allow you to experiment with formats, explore innovative ideas, and reach your audience in ways that were previously unthinkable. AI is not here to replace the human touch but to amplify it. Thanks to its suggestions, you can refine your ideas and find new inspiration, drawing from an intelligence that learns and evolves alongside you.

Start by regularly publishing articles and videos using these tools, creating a coherent and captivating narrative for your audience. Over time, you will not only see growing interest around your content, but you can also turn this passion into a source of income. Monetizing your blog or channel will become a tangible possibility through advertisements, sponsorships, or selling products and services related to your brand.

What matters, in the end, is not just the quantity of content you produce, but the quality and impact it has on your audience. AI can help you find that perfect balance between innovation and authenticity, saving you time and resources without ever compromising the value of what you share. Leveraging these technologies means not just keeping pace with the times but becoming part of a future where creative intelligence is enhanced by tools that amplify its potential.

2.3.2 Earning Opportunities with Dropshipping and AI

A New Horizon for Digital Entrepreneurs

Dropshipping represents one of the most accessible opportunities to start an online business without the need to physically manage inventory. This business model not only eliminates the risks associated with storage costs but also allows you to focus on strategic aspects of the business, such as product selection and brand building. By integrating artificial intelligence (AI) into your dropshipping approach, you can amplify your earning potential and create a highly personalized shopping experience.

Discovering Trending Products with AI
One of the biggest advantages of AI in dropshipping is its ability to analyze data and identify market trends in real-time. Tools like Oberlo not only simplify the search for products to sell but also use advanced algorithms to analyze sales, user behavior, and customer reviews. This analysis allows you to identify the most sought-after products, enabling you to quickly adapt your offerings and position yourself competitively in the market.

Personalizing the Shopping Experience
AI can transform the shopping experience, making it more interactive and engaging for customers. Through

machine learning technologies, you can offer personalized recommendations based on users' previous shopping habits. This not only increases the likelihood of sales but also helps build a relationship of trust and loyalty with the customer. Personalization can also extend to communication, allowing you to send targeted marketing emails and special offers that resonate with each customer's specific interests.

Optimizing Marketing and Sales
In the context of dropshipping, AI is not limited to supporting research and personalization; it can also significantly enhance marketing strategies. Artificial intelligence tools can analyze the performance data of your advertising campaigns, providing insights into which strategies work best. This information allows you to optimize your advertising budget, refine your messaging, and identify the most effective channels to reach your target audience.

Moreover, e-commerce platforms like Shopify offer integrated apps that leverage AI to analyze user behavior on your site. These apps can suggest changes to layout, content, and even offers based on buyer behavior analysis, thereby improving the effectiveness of your sales.

Scalability and Sustainable Growth
One of the great advantages of dropshipping is its scalability. As your business grows, AI can help you manage the increasing volume of sales and customer interactions without the need to invest in additional human resources. You can automate daily operations, such as order processing and customer service management, freeing up valuable time to focus on strategy and brand expansion.

Dropshipping combined with artificial intelligence offers an unprecedented array of opportunities for those looking to start an online business. It not only allows you to launch a business with low startup costs but also provides you with powerful tools to analyze, personalize, and optimize every aspect of your operation. With a well-defined strategy and an innovative approach, dropshipping can evolve into a significant and sustainable source of income over time. It is not just an earning opportunity; it is a journey of discovery, learning, and growth in the dynamic landscape of e-commerce.

Chapter 3

AI and Marketing: Reaching Your Audience

In an increasingly digital world, artificial intelligence (AI) offers powerful tools to help businesses understand their audience and optimize marketing strategies. In this chapter, we will explore how AI can transform the way we interact with customers, creating opportunities for more effective and personalized advertising campaigns.

3.1 Understanding Customer Data with AI

3.1.1 How AI Analyzes Consumer Behavior

Data analysis is fundamental to understanding consumer behavior. AI can examine vast amounts of data in seconds, identifying patterns and trends that might elude manual analysis. Using machine learning techniques, AI can analyze user interactions with your website, emails, and social media, providing valuable insights into their behavior.

For example, tools like Google Analytics and Hotjar offer insights into the time users spend on specific pages and the actions they take. This data will allow you to understand which products or services attract your customers the most, thereby refining your marketing strategies.

3.1.2 Using Insights to Improve Sales

Once data is collected, the next step is to use it to enhance sales. With AI, you can segment your audience based on specific behaviors, creating personalized offers for each group. For instance, if you notice that a group of customers frequently purchases fashion items, you can send them targeted newsletters with exclusive discounts on new arrivals.

Moreover, AI can predict future trends by analyzing historical data. This enables you to adapt your marketing strategies in real-time, anticipating your customers' needs and maximizing sales opportunities.

3.2 Personalized Marketing Strategies

3.2.1 Creating Targeted Advertising Campaigns

AI allows you to create highly targeted advertising campaigns. By using advertising tools like Facebook Ads and Google Ads, you can set up campaigns that reach only your ideal audience. For example, you can segment your target based on interests, purchasing behavior, and demographic data.

Thanks to these features, your campaigns will be more effective, reducing budget waste and increasing conversion rates. Targeted advertising campaigns not only attract more customers but also build stronger relationships with existing ones.

3.2.2 Practical Examples of Personalization with AI

A clear example of how artificial intelligence can transform the shopping experience is represented by recommendation systems. These algorithms, used by e-commerce giants like Amazon, analyze past purchasing behaviors and user preferences to suggest products that may interest them. It's not just about showing similar items, but creating a deeper, more personalized connection with the customer.

By implementing a recommendation system in your business, you can not only increase the likelihood of cross-selling—suggesting relevant accessories to a main product—but also improve up-selling by presenting higher-end or complementary versions of the product the customer is considering.

For instance, if a customer buys a camera, your system might suggest purchasing compatible lenses, carrying bags, or extended warranty services. This approach not only enhances the shopping experience, making the process smoother and more satisfying, but can also significantly increase the average order value.

Furthermore, AI can analyze data in real-time to continuously optimize recommendations. By adapting to emerging purchasing trends and changes in user behavior, the system becomes increasingly effective, contributing to creating a virtuous cycle of customer loyalty and sales growth. In this way, personalization is not just an aesthetic innovation but a fundamental strategy to drive business growth.

3.3 Competitors in Digital Marketing: Google and Its Solutions

3.3.1 Google's automated marketing tools

Google is a leader in digital marketing, offering a wide range of automated tools to optimize advertising campaigns. Platforms like Google Ads and Google Analytics provide valuable data to analyze the performance of your campaigns, allowing you to make informed decisions.

Additionally, tools like Google Optimize allow you to test different variants of your web pages to discover which performs best. With automation, you can save time and effort, enabling you to focus on other strategic areas of your business.

3.3.2 Case Study: Companies that Have Benefited from Google's AI

Numerous companies have benefited from using Google's marketing tools. For instance, a small e-commerce business used Google Ads to create targeted advertising campaigns. By analyzing the campaign data, it optimized its ads, increasing ROI (return on investment) by 150% within a few months.

Another example is a marketing agency that integrated Google Analytics into its operations. By analyzing customer behavior, it was able to refine its email marketing strategies, achieving a 30% increase in email open rates. These examples demonstrate how AI and Google's tools can radically transform marketing performance, even for small businesses.

Chapter 4

Creativity Enhanced by AI

After exploring how artificial intelligence can improve marketing, it's time to consider another crucial aspect: creativity. AI is not just a tool for analysis and automation; it is becoming an indispensable collaborator for artists, writers, musicians, and content creators. In this chapter, we will see how AI is transforming the way we create content, from articles to music, to videos and media.

4.1 Generating Creative Content

4.1.1 Writing Articles and Stories with AI

AI has made significant strides in generating written content. Tools like ChatGPT and Jasper enable anyone to create articles, stories, and even novels quickly and easily. Thanks to natural language processing (NLP), these platforms can generate coherent and well-structured texts based on specific input.

For example, if you're writing a travel blog, you can ask an AI app to generate an article on the best destinations for 2024. By simply entering a few keywords, the AI will produce an informative text that you can review and edit. This technology not only saves time but also offers fresh and innovative ideas, expanding your creativity.

4.1.2 Creating Art and Design with AI Tools

AI is not limited to writing; it is also revolutionizing the field of art and design. Platforms like DALL-E and DeepArt allow users to generate artwork simply by entering textual descriptions. These tools use deep learning algorithms to create unique images that reflect your ideas.

Imagine you want to create a book cover. You can describe the atmosphere, colors, and desired subjects, and the AI will provide several artistic options. This not only broadens creative possibilities but also makes art accessible to those without specific design training.

4.2 Music and Video: AI as a Collaborator

4.2.1 Composing Songs with AI

Music is another area where AI is making remarkable progress. Tools like Amper Music and AIVA are designed to help musicians compose original tracks. These tools analyze millions of existing songs to understand musical structures and melodies, enabling high-quality music creation in minutes.

If you're a beginner musician, you can use AI to generate melodies or instrumental accompaniments. By adding your personal touch and lyrics, you can produce complete songs without having to master advanced music theory.

4.2.2 Automatically Editing Videos: How to Do It

Video creation has become simpler thanks to AI. Platforms like Magisto and Lumen5 offer tools that automatically edit videos based on the clips and images you upload. You can simply enter the text, and the AI will select the best moments, apply transitions, and add background music.

This is particularly useful for content creators who want to maintain a steady flow of videos on social media without spending hours in post-production. With AI, video content creation becomes accessible and less intimidating, allowing anyone to express their creativity.

4.3 AI in Media Production

4.3.1 Examples of Companies Using AI in Media

Many of the leading names in the media industry are already integrating AI into their processes. Netflix, for example, uses AI-based recommendation algorithms to suggest content to users by analyzing their preferences and viewing behavior. This has led to a significant increase in engagement and customer satisfaction.

Another example is The Washington Post, which uses AI to automatically generate sports articles and real-time event reports. These tools allow for the production of fresh and relevant content quickly, keeping users informed without delays.

4.3.2 How Creators Are Leveraging AI
Content creators are embracing AI to enhance their productivity and the quality of their work. For example, many YouTubers use AI-based video editing tools to speed up the editing process, while bloggers and writers use content generation tools to fill gaps in their creative ideas.

Moreover, content personalization has become a key strategy for creators. By utilizing analytics data provided by AI, creators can better understand their audience and tailor their content based on viewer preferences, increasing engagement and loyalty.

Chapter 5

AI for Personal and Professional Improvement

5.1 AI-Based Learning Tools

Artificial intelligence (AI) has revolutionized many sectors, and personal and professional improvement is no exception. With its ability to personalize learning and adapt to individual needs, AI offers extraordinary opportunities for acquiring new skills, improving performance, and driving change in daily life. We will explore how AI is applied in education, skill development, and personal growth.

5.1.1 Educational Platforms Utilizing AI

AI is radically changing the educational landscape by improving access to learning and making it more engaging. Several platforms use advanced algorithms to personalize the experience and help students progress at their own pace. Some of the most notable ones include:

- **Coursera:** A leading platform offering courses in collaboration with prestigious institutions. Coursera's AI analyzes student performance, suggesting additional resources and adapting content to individual progress.
- **Duolingo:** Specializing in language learning, Duolingo uses AI algorithms to personalize exercises and monitor areas where users struggle, as well as leveraging voice recognition technologies to improve pronunciation.
- **Khan Academy:** With virtual tutors, AI identifies learning gaps and offers suggestions for improvement, allowing students to learn at their own pace.
- **LinkedIn Learning:** A professional development platform that uses AI to recommend courses based on users' skills and career goals, tracking progress and suggesting continuous updates.

- **MasterClass:** Offers courses from world-renowned experts and utilizes AI to recommend personalized content, enhancing users' learning experiences.

5.1.2 How AI Personalizes the Learning Experience

The most revolutionary aspect of AI in education is its ability to adapt the experience in real-time, customizing content and pace. AI acts as an invisible mentor, collecting data on student behavior to optimize learning paths.

- **Behavioral Data Analysis**
    - **Progress Tracking:** AI monitors student performance, identifying weak points and suggesting targeted exercises to improve skills.
    - **Adaptive Learning:** If a student struggles with a topic, AI presents content differently or provides additional resources.
    - **Preference Identification:** AI can recognize a student's preferred format, such as video or quizzes, thus personalizing the learning experience.
- **Content and Pace Adaptation**
  AI adapts the pace and content of courses based on individual capabilities, offering a more efficient learning experience:
    - **Personalized Pace:** Allows students to learn at different speeds, avoiding frustration or boredom.
    - **Personalized Content:** Proposes additional materials to reinforce understanding and accelerates the curriculum for those who have already acquired the necessary knowledge.
- **Emotional Intelligence and Learning**
  AI can detect students' emotional states, such as frustration or confusion, and respond accordingly:
    - **Emotion Detection:** Using advanced algorithms, AI can analyze facial

expressions or voice tone to adjust teaching methods.
    - **Motivating Environment:** Through positive feedback and virtual rewards, AI helps keep students motivated.
- **AI-Mediated Collaborative Learning**
  AI also facilitates collaborative learning by creating virtual study groups based on complementary skills and common interests:
    - **Study Group Creation:** Fosters collaboration among students with similar profiles.
    - **Group Project Moderation:** AI moderates and guides group work, resolving conflicts and suggesting useful resources.

Continuous Learning and Personalization Beyond the Course

AI is not limited to a specific course but continues to provide recommendations even after completion, suggesting new courses or projects to keep learning alive.

5.2 Skill Development with AI

5.2.1 Continuous Training Through Intelligent Tools

AI is a fundamental resource for continuous training, especially in a rapidly evolving work environment. It enables the improvement of technical and soft skills in a self-directed and flexible manner.

Self-Learning and Cognitive Intelligence
AI allows for dynamic learning, adapting training paths to the user's specific needs:

- **Dynamic Learning Paths:** AI modifies the learning pathway based on student results, speeding up or slowing down the pace.

- **Predictive Feedback:** AI can anticipate future difficulties and intervene proactively with additional resources.

Immersive Training and Simulated Experiences
Thanks to integration with virtual reality (VR) and augmented reality (AR), AI enables immersive experiences:

- **Complex Simulations:** AI recreates realistic scenarios to train users in safe virtual contexts.
- **Immersive Learning:** With VR and AR, users can interact in three-dimensional worlds and improve their skills practically.

Continuous Learning and Personal Growth Curve
AI promotes long-term learning by providing personalized recommendations and fostering the development of soft skills:

- **Long-Term Recommendations:** Suggests new courses or skills to learn based on progress made.
- **Digital Mentoring:** Provides personalized advice to guide the user's career choices.

5.3 Philosophy and Personal Growth: AI as a Guide

5.3.1 AI for Improving Daily Life
Artificial intelligence is transforming our daily lives, not only from a technical standpoint but also in terms of personal growth and well-being improvement. Through a variety of tools and applications, AI offers unique opportunities to optimize our daily routines, freeing up precious time and increasing productivity.

Optimization of Daily Tasks
One of the most relevant aspects of AI is its ability to simplify daily activities. Virtual assistants like Siri, Google Assistant, and Alexa not only answer questions and provide information but also help

manage tasks by setting reminders, organizing events, and facilitating communication. This automation allows users to focus their energies on more meaningful and rewarding tasks, reducing stress related to planning and time management.

Moreover, AI-powered time management applications can analyze our work habits and suggest strategies to improve efficiency. These tools can identify peak productivity times and recommend techniques like the Pomodoro method, which encourages regular breaks to maintain high levels of focus and creativity. This approach not only enhances productivity but also contributes to greater personal satisfaction, as people feel more in control of their days.

Improvement of Interpersonal Relationships
AI also has the potential to positively influence interpersonal relationships. Through data analysis algorithms, some platforms can suggest ways to improve communication with friends and family, providing prompts for meaningful conversations or helping to remember special events and birthdays. Additionally, AI can facilitate connections between people with similar interests, creating communities and support networks that promote social well-being.

Management of Personal Resources
Another crucial aspect of AI in daily life is its ability to assist in managing personal resources, such as money and time. Intelligent financial tools can analyze spending and provide personalized recommendations to improve budget management, allowing for more effective financial planning. This not only reduces anxiety related to financial management but also promotes greater accountability and awareness regarding spending habits.

In the health sphere, apps and wearable devices can monitor vital parameters, physical activity, and eating habits, providing real-time feedback and personalized suggestions for a healthier lifestyle. This integration of AI into health management not only helps people take care of their bodies but also encourages a proactive mindset towards well-being, fostering personal growth.

As AI technologies evolve, it is essential to also consider the ethical and social implications. While AI offers undeniable advantages, it is crucial to reflect on its impact on privacy and personal autonomy. As technologies become increasingly integrated into our daily lives, balancing comfort and safety becomes vital.

Artificial intelligence represents a powerful tool for improving daily life, optimizing activities, enhancing productivity, and promoting personal growth. The key to success lies in using these technologies consciously and responsibly, integrating them into our lives in ways that maximize benefits and minimize risks. Only then can we fully harness the transformative potential of AI, not only to improve our efficiency but also to enrich our overall human experience.

5.3.2 AI as a Tool for Self-Discovery and Improvement

Artificial intelligence is emerging as a powerful ally in the journey of self-discovery and personal improvement. Thanks to its ability to process and analyze large volumes of data, AI offers tools and resources that can transform our understanding of ourselves and our potential.

One of the most interesting aspects of AI is its capacity to facilitate personal reflection through the use of emotional intelligence technologies. These tools can analyze our emotions and moods, guiding us through a process of introspection. For example, AI-supported journaling applications can pose specific and thought-provoking questions, encouraging us to explore our thoughts and feelings more deeply.

These guided reflections can contribute to greater self-awareness, allowing us to identify behavioral patterns, personal values, and areas for improvement. AI can also provide personalized feedback, helping us recognize our strengths and the challenges we need to address, facilitating a continuous process of self-assessment.

Support for Continuous Growth
In addition to promoting personal reflection, AI acts as a virtual coach, providing personalized suggestions and prompts for personal growth. By using machine learning algorithms, these applications can analyze our daily activities, habits, and progress in achieving goals, offering specific and targeted recommendations.

For instance, an intelligent fitness app could suggest personalized exercises based on our recent progress, while an online learning platform could recommend courses or resources that align with our interests and professional aspirations. This ongoing support encourages continuous improvement, pushing us to surpass our limits and explore new opportunities.

Furthermore, AI can facilitate the tracking of our emotions and moods over time, offering a clear picture of our emotional well-being. Through detailed analyses and personalized reports, we can make more informed and conscious decisions regarding our personal growth, thereby enhancing our quality of life.

Integration with Other Growth Tools
Another advantage of AI in the field of self-discovery is its ability to integrate with other tools and resources for personal development. For example, it can collaborate with meditation apps, time management tools, or professional networking platforms to provide a holistic approach to growth. This synergy allows us to tackle challenges from multiple angles, enhancing our ability to adapt to change and new circumstances.

Artificial intelligence emerges as a valuable tool for self-discovery and personal improvement, offering support and guidance on a journey that requires commitment, introspection, and openness to change.

With the aid of advanced technologies, we can explore our potential in new and meaningful ways, contributing to a continuous process of personal growth and development.

Chapter 6

AI in the Financial Sector: Earning Smartly

The financial sector has been transformed by artificial intelligence, which has not only made processes more efficient but also opened new opportunities for investment and personal finance management. This chapter will explore how AI can be used to enhance financial data analysis, automate personal finances, and democratize investments.

6.1 Financial Data Analysis with AI

Financial data analysis is essential for making informed decisions. AI offers tools and technologies that can significantly improve this analysis, making it more accurate and timely.

6.1.1 How AI Can Help Make Better Investments

AI can analyze enormous volumes of data in real-time, identifying patterns and trends that might escape human attention. For example, machine learning algorithms can predict stock market movements by analyzing factors such as:

- **Historical Data**: AI can examine past stock performance, highlighting correlations and anomalies.
- **Sentiment Analysis**: By analyzing news, social media, and financial reports, AI can gauge market sentiment, providing insights into how investor emotions influence price fluctuations.
- **Predictive Analysis**: Using advanced statistical models, AI can make predictions based on economic, political, and social variables, allowing investors to anticipate market changes.

Investors and traders should consider integrating AI-based tools into their strategies. Using platforms that offer AI-based analysis can enhance their ability to make informed and timely decisions.

6.1.2 User-Friendly Financial Analysis Tools

With technological advancements, numerous AI-based financial analysis tools are available that are accessible even to non-experts. Some examples include:

- **Automated Trading Platforms**: These tools use algorithms to execute trades based on predefined criteria, reducing the need for constant monitoring.
- **Analysis Dashboards**: Tools like Tableau or Power BI, powered by AI, can transform financial data into intuitive visualizations, making information easier to interpret.

It is beneficial to choose tools that not only offer powerful analytical capabilities but are also user-friendly and integrable with other financial applications already in use.

6.2 Automation of Personal Finances

Automation is one of the areas where AI has had a significant impact, improving personal finance management.

6.2.1 Apps That Manage Daily Expenses

Numerous apps, such as Mint or YNAB (You Need A Budget), use AI to help users monitor expenses and manage budgets. These tools offer features such as:

- **Expense Analysis**: Automatic identification of categorized expenses, allowing users to better understand where their money goes.
- **Custom Alerts**: Automatic notifications when certain spending limits are reached, helping maintain control over finances.

Using a finance management app can reduce the stress associated with monitoring daily expenses, making budget planning simpler.

6.2.2 Optimizing Savings and Investments with AI

In addition to expense management, AI can help optimize savings and investments. Some tools offer:

- **Investment Recommendations**: Based on the analysis of spending habits and financial goals, they can suggest personalized investment portfolios.
- **Automated Savings Plans**: Apps like Digit use AI to analyze spending and automatically transfer small amounts of money into a savings account, optimizing the accumulation process.

Setting clear financial goals and using AI tools to monitor and optimize progress towards these goals can lead to a significant improvement in long-term financial health.

6.3 Competitors in the Sector: Robinhood and Investment Accessibility

The emergence of platforms like Robinhood has radically changed the investment landscape, making it more accessible to a broader audience.

6.3.1 How Robinhood Changed the Way We Invest

In the modern investment landscape, Robinhood has emerged as a catalyst for change, revolutionizing the traditional approach to trading and making participation in financial markets more democratic and accessible. Founded in 2013 by Vladimir Tenev and Baiju Bhatt, Robinhood leveraged technology to break down barriers that previously limited investment access to a narrow elite, primarily consisting of institutional investors and wealthy individuals. The platform's core philosophy is that "access to finance is a right, not a privilege," and this principle has guided its mission from the beginning.

One of the most significant turning points that Robinhood introduced was the elimination of trading commissions. Traditionally, trading stocks and financial instruments involved significant costs, with brokerage fees weighing on buy and sell transactions. This business model discouraged many potential investors, especially those belonging to younger generations or lower-income groups, who might not have the resources to cover such expenses. With the introduction of a completely commission-free platform, Robinhood made trading stocks and cryptocurrencies a realistic option for anyone with even a modest initial capital.

Robinhood's user interface is another element that has contributed to its popularity. The design is intended to be intuitive and user-friendly, making the trading experience easy even for those approaching the investment world for the first time. With just a few clicks, users can buy and sell stocks, monitor their investment performance, and access real-time market information. This simplicity not only makes trading more accessible but also encourages new investors to explore market opportunities without the fear of facing a complex or intimidating platform.

The democratization of investing has attracted an extraordinary number of new users, particularly among younger generations like Millennials and Gen Z. These generations, raised in an era of increasing digitization and with a strong sense of self-determination, have felt inspired to take control of their finances. The easy access to the information and resources needed to make investment decisions enables them to actively participate in the markets, in contrast to the perception that investments are reserved for experts or those with considerable financial resources.

Another innovation that Robinhood introduced is the ability to invest in fractional shares. This means that even investors with limited capital can purchase a portion of a company's share rather than having to invest the entire value of a single share. This option has made it possible to invest in high-value stocks, such as those of large technology companies, even for those who do not have a substantial capital base. In this way, Robinhood has further reduced entry barriers and promoted a more inclusive investment culture.

However, the exponential growth of Robinhood and similar platforms has also raised some concerns. The simplicity and accessibility of trading can encourage speculative behavior, with users venturing into high-risk investments without a proper understanding of market dynamics. In a context where financial information is easily accessible but often superficial or misunderstood, there is a risk that less experienced investors may make decisions based on emotions rather than fundamental analysis. The speed at which the market can move, combined with the ability to make instant trades via an app, has led some critics to emphasize the need for stronger financial education for investors to navigate the investment world responsibly.

Moreover, the growing influence of Robinhood has led to significant changes in how other trading platforms operate. Traditional institutions have had to adapt to this new competitive landscape by changing their cost policies and investing in technologies to enhance user experience. This has contributed to an overall decrease in commissions in the sector, allowing even more people to access financial markets.

The impact of Robinhood extends beyond mere trading. The platform has created an active community of investors who share ideas, strategies, and successes. Through social media and online forums, users can compare notes, learn from each other, and engage in discussions about investments and market trends. This exchange of information has contributed to the formation of a new generation of more informed and active investors, ready to use their knowledge to navigate a complex and ever-evolving financial environment.

Robinhood has marked a significant turning point in the investment world, democratizing access to markets and making stock and cryptocurrency trading more appealing and accessible to a wider audience. Its innovative proposition has inspired a cultural and practical shift in how individuals perceive and approach investments. While the challenges associated with this new trading model are evident, the potential for improved financial education and for active, informed participation in the markets is stronger than ever. The story of Robinhood is just beginning, but it is already emerging as an emblematic example of how technology can radically change the economic and social dynamics of our era.

6.3.2 Democratized Investment Opportunities with AI

Artificial intelligence (AI) has opened the doors to a new paradigm in the world of investments, radically transforming how people approach financial markets. It not only provides advanced tools and resources that were once the exclusive domain of professional investors but also democratizes access to crucial information, making investing a more inclusive and accessible activity for everyone. With the integration of AI, investment platforms are redefining trading dynamics, creating an ecosystem where every investor, regardless of their experience, can navigate and thrive.

One of the most exciting opportunities that AI brings is the ability to offer personalized recommendations. By utilizing sophisticated algorithms and predictive analytics, AI-powered investment platforms can monitor users' preferences, behaviors, and performance to provide tailored suggestions. These suggestions can range from specific investment strategies to identifying market opportunities, allowing investors to make more informed and targeted decisions. With constant analysis of market data and economic trends, AI enables the adaptation of investment strategies in real-time, ensuring that users can maximize their gains and minimize risks.

In this context, education and information play a fundamental role. AI-based investment platforms not only provide recommendations but also offer educational resources that help users understand market dynamics and investment strategies. Online courses, webinars, and interactive tutorials are just some of the ways through which AI facilitates learning. Investors, even those who are beginners, can access valuable knowledge that previously required years of experience or formal studies. This ongoing education allows an increasing number of individuals to enter the markets with greater confidence and awareness.

Another crucial aspect of AI in the investment world is the democratization of analytical tools. Advanced data analysis technologies and market resources were once reserved for financial institutions and industry professionals. Today, thanks to AI, even non-professional investors can access sophisticated analytical tools. Intuitive dashboards, interactive charts, and detailed reports are now just a click away. This access to advanced analytical tools enables investors to monitor their performance, assess market trends, and make informed decisions based on concrete data. The ability to utilize these resources can make the difference between a mediocre investment and a truly profitable one.

Artificial intelligence technology does not only provide analytical tools and recommendations; it also promotes the automation of personal finances. Applications that integrate AI can help users manage their daily finances, plan budgets, track expenses, and even set savings goals. With automation, individuals can optimize their finances without dedicating hours to planning. The ability to manage finances efficiently frees up time and resources, allowing users to focus on more strategic and profitable investments.

The impact of AI does not stop here. Its application in the financial sector goes beyond simple analysis and investment management. Emerging technologies, such as robo-advisors, use advanced algorithms to manage investment portfolios, offering personalized advice at significantly lower costs compared to traditional advisors. This automated approach allows for the diversification of investments and risk reduction, making financial advice accessible to a broader range of people. The transparency of costs and ease of use are elements that attract investors of all ages, promoting greater participation in the market.

The integration of AI into the investment landscape also leads to the creation of more sophisticated investment strategies. Algorithms can analyze vast volumes of data in real-time, identifying patterns and trends that might escape even the most experienced analysts. This data-driven approach not only increases the likelihood of investment success but also helps mitigate risks associated with impulsive or emotional decisions. The ability to analyze and interpret data quickly and efficiently represents a paradigm shift in the world of investments, where artificial intelligence serves as a strategic ally.

Moreover, AI is contributing to greater accountability and sustainability in the investment sector. Intelligent platforms can analyze not only financial data but also environmental, social, and governance (ESG) factors, enabling investors to make more conscious decisions aligned with their values. This growing focus on sustainable investing is driving a new era of social responsibility in business, where ethics and sustainability become key priorities for investors.

Artificial intelligence is radically changing the investment landscape, making tools and resources once reserved for the privileged few accessible to all. Thanks to the personalization of recommendations, continuous education, and advanced analysis, even novice investors can make more informed and conscious decisions. With AI facilitating financial management and promoting a sustainable approach, the future of investments looks bright, inclusive, and, above all, ever-evolving. The real opportunity lies in integrating these technologies into one's investment strategy, enabling smarter and more informed earning. In this way, every individual has the chance to become not just a consumer but an active and informed investor in the financial world.

Chapter 7
The Future of AI: Opportunities and Challenges

As we venture into the future of artificial intelligence, we find ourselves facing a landscape rich in opportunities and challenges. AI has the potential to revolutionize every aspect of our lives, from work and education to health. However, with these possibilities arise fundamental questions regarding ethics, accountability, and the skills needed to navigate this new world. In this chapter, we will explore not only what lies ahead but also how we can prepare for a future where AI plays a central role.

7.1 Future Perspectives for Artificial Intelligence

7.1.1 Emerging Sectors Where AI Will Have a Significant Impact

Artificial intelligence (AI) is rapidly shaping the future of numerous sectors, bringing unprecedented innovations and transformations. While AI has already begun to show its potential in established sectors such as healthcare, transportation, and marketing, the real explosion of its capabilities will occur in emerging sectors. Among these, environmental sustainability and biotechnology stand out as two crucial frontiers where AI could have a significant impact, not only to improve efficiency but also to address some of the most urgent challenges of our time.

In the context of environmental sustainability, AI presents itself as a powerful tool capable of analyzing vast volumes of environmental data. Imagine a network of sensors distributed across the planet, collecting real-time information on temperature, air quality, humidity, and natural resource use. By analyzing this data, AI can identify patterns and trends, offering personalized solutions for the sustainable management of resources. For example, an AI system could monitor the water reserves of a region and suggest optimal irrigation strategies, avoiding waste and ensuring equitable distribution of drinking water, a precious and increasingly scarce resource.

But sustainability is not limited to water resource management. AI can also play a crucial role in reducing carbon emissions. Through predictive analysis, AI can optimize transport routes, reducing fuel consumption and, consequently, greenhouse gas emissions. Imagine fleets of autonomous vehicles coordinated by an intelligent system that chooses the most efficient routes in real time, minimizing environmental impact. This could not only contribute to more sustainable mobility but also revolutionize the entire transportation sector, creating a future where reducing the ecological footprint becomes a primary goal.

In biotechnology, AI is set to revolutionize how we develop drugs and medical treatments. Traditionally, drug discovery is a lengthy, costly process with relatively low success rates. The introduction of AI in this field could significantly shorten development times. By using advanced algorithms and machine learning, AI can analyze vast datasets of genomic and clinical data to identify potential candidates for new drugs and optimize clinical trials. Imagine a world where researchers can leverage the computing power of AI to simulate thousands of molecular interactions in just a few days, identifying promising compounds and accelerating the approval process. This speed could make a difference between life and death for many individuals.

Moreover, AI could contribute to a more personalized approach to medicine. By analyzing genetic and clinical data, treatments could be specifically tailored to each patient's needs, paving the way for personalized therapies that address diseases more effectively. This approach would not only increase the likelihood of treatment success but also reduce side effects, improving patients' quality of life.

Biotechnology, combined with AI, could not only accelerate drug discovery but also improve outcomes for patients, revolutionizing the healthcare sector.

However, as AI expands into these emerging sectors, critical questions arise about how to ensure that these technologies are used for the common good. In a world where resources are increasingly concentrated in the hands of a few, it is essential to ask who will benefit from these innovations. If AI in biotechnology can lead to revolutionary discoveries in health, its accessibility and distribution remain crucial points of concern. There is a risk that advancements in these fields could be exploited solely for the profit of certain companies or individuals, rather than for the collective good.

Additionally, environmental sustainability must become a priority rather than an option. AI-based technologies need to be implemented with a long-term vision, keeping in mind the need to preserve our planet for future generations. It is vital to promote a culture of responsible innovation, where ethics play a central role in the design and implementation of these technologies.

The capacity of AI to transform sustainability and biotechnology is palpable, and the potential is immense. However, the challenges ahead require deep reflection and careful planning to ensure that benefits are equitably distributed and that technology serves everyone, not just a privileged few. In this context, dialogue among scientists, politicians, entrepreneurs, and citizens becomes essential to define ethical guidelines and policies that will govern the use of AI in emerging sectors, ensuring that these potentials are harnessed for a fairer and more sustainable future.

7.1.2 Preparing for a Future Dominated by AI

Preparing for a future dominated by artificial intelligence does not simply mean acquiring new technical skills; it implies a radical shift in our mindset and approach to both professional and personal life. In an era where technology is advancing at an unprecedented pace, the ability to adapt and respond to these changes becomes fundamental. Continuous learning emerges as an essential necessity, no longer just an option, but a true survival strategy in the world of work.

Starting a learning journey is not limited to following traditional courses; it means exploring a variety of educational forms that fit our lifestyle and needs. Online courses, webinars, informative podcasts, and digital resources are becoming increasingly accessible. Platforms like Coursera, edX, and Udacity offer learning opportunities on topics such as AI, machine learning, data management, and much more. Imagine being able to learn directly from industry experts and university professors without even having to leave the comfort of your home. Every completed course represents a step forward toward understanding emerging technologies, opening new doors and opportunities.

However, formal learning is only part of the equation. It is also crucial to develop an adaptable and resilient mindset. The challenges of the future will require not only technical skills but also problem-solving abilities, critical thinking, and creativity. This means cultivating curiosity and the desire to explore new fields. Participating in learning communities, both physical and virtual, can be an effective way to stay updated on emerging trends. These communities provide the opportunity to engage with people from diverse backgrounds and areas of expertise, stimulating dialogue and the sharing of innovative ideas.

Networking with industry professionals is another key piece in preparing for a future dominated by AI. Building a network of contacts not only helps to discover job opportunities but can also provide valuable insights into market evolutions. Attending conferences, seminars, and industry events allows you to connect with thought leaders and innovators. These interactions can be inspiring and open your mind to new possibilities. Imagine exchanging ideas with someone developing a new AI application or with an entrepreneur innovating in a completely different field. Every conversation has the potential to spark a creative idea that could lead to new initiatives.

Moreover, the importance of investing in personal development cannot be underestimated. Readers are encouraged to consider dedicating time to new areas of interest that may not be immediately related to their current profession but could prove valuable in the future. This process of personal discovery could include writing, art, programming, or even entrepreneurship. Openness to new experiences and learning opportunities can transform a career path, creating a more versatile and adaptable profile capable of tackling the challenges and opportunities presented by AI.

The future offers us a blank canvas on which to paint our aspirations. Preparing for this future means not just being passive spectators, but becoming active participants in change. Every step taken toward learning and personal growth contributes to building a repertoire of skills that will allow us to navigate the complex and ever-evolving landscape of artificial intelligence. In a world where technology continues to change the rules of the game, being proactive and engaged in our development can make the difference between falling behind and leading the change. The choice to invest in ourselves and our skills is not just a personal decision, but an opportunity to shape a future in which AI and humanity can coexist harmoniously and productively.

7.2 Ethics and Responsibility in AI Use

7.2.1 Philosophical Reflections on Ethics and Technology

The emergence of AI prompts us to reflect on fundamental ethical questions. What are the moral implications of automated decisions? Who is responsible when an algorithm makes a wrong decision? These questions require deep consideration and open discussion. Each of us should ask ourselves about our relationship with technology. It is essential not only to understand how AI works but also to reflect on how we want it to be used. In an age where machines can influence people's lives, collective responsibility becomes essential.

7.2.2 The Importance of Responsibility in the Adoption of AI

The adoption of AI must be guided by principles of responsibility and transparency. Companies and developers must be aware of the impact of their technologies and commit to ensuring that AI is used ethically. Let's reflect on how we can be conscious consumers and support responsible business practices. Our voice matters: we can demand greater transparency and accountability from companies that use AI.

7.3 Preparing for Imminent Changes

7.3.1 Required Skills in the Future Labor Market

The emergence of artificial intelligence is reshaping the labor landscape in ways we could have never imagined. In this evolving context, traditional skills are no longer sufficient; there is a growing need for new and distinctive abilities. Critical thinking and creativity take center stage, becoming essential tools for solving complex problems and generating innovation. The ability to collaborate with machines and adapt to ever-evolving technologies is not just an advantage but a true imperative. It is vital to reflect on one's skills and assess the areas where growth is possible. Embracing a mindset of continuous learning not only prepares us to navigate a constantly changing job market but also enriches our personal and professional journey. Investing in our development means being ready to face future challenges and seize unexpected opportunities.

7.3.2 How to Remain Competitive in an Evolving World

Remaining competitive in a rapidly evolving world requires a proactive attitude and considerable flexibility. It is no longer enough to acquire new skills; it is essential to be open to new and unexpected experiences. Building solid and meaningful professional networks becomes crucial. Collaboration, in fact, proves fundamental in creating opportunities, allowing access to a wide range of perspectives and ideas that can enrich one's work. In this context, support networks and professional communities are not just tools, but true catalysts for growth. They amplify opportunities, making the professional journey not only more dynamic but also more rewarding and meaningful. Embracing change and diversity is not just a competitive advantage but a key to innovation and resilience. In a constantly transforming world, those who can adapt and collaborate will not only survive but thrive, creating a professional future rich with possibilities.

Chapter 8

Earnings and the Transformation of the World

8.1 A Future to Govern Wisely

Artificial intelligence (AI) has long surpassed the boundary between science fiction and reality, asserting itself as one of the most powerful agents of transformation in the modern world. Its applications are everywhere, from industrial automation to personalizing user experiences, to financial services that leverage its ability to process vast amounts of data to make predictive decisions. However, like any technological revolution, this great wave of change is not without risks. In this concluding chapter, we will reflect on the deeper aspects of the ongoing transformation, exploring the potential risks to humanity, the fiscal regulation of earnings linked to artificial intelligence, and the current regulatory framework that seeks to govern this extraordinary innovation.

8.1.1 The Challenge of Human Change

One of the most pressing questions raised by AI is its impact on human identity and social structure. As technology advances at breakneck speed, we must confront a new reality in which many traditional activities, from work to creativity, can be performed more effectively by intelligent machines. This phenomenon raises a crucial question: what does it mean to be human in a world where intelligence is no longer an exclusively human trait?

The speed at which AI is integrating into our daily lives is astonishing. It has not only begun to replace some job tasks but has also started to influence deep aspects of our creativity and personal expression. Consider, for example, algorithm-generated art, which can produce visual, musical, and literary works with a level of sophistication that we would have previously considered exclusively human. If a machine can generate a painting that evokes emotions similar to a Van Gogh work or a musical piece that resonates with the same intensity as a Beethoven symphony, we face an unprecedented intellectual and philosophical challenge. The ability to create, one of humanity's defining characteristics, is thus called into question.

But AI does not simply replace manual or creative tasks; it also modifies our conception of work and value. Work, traditionally seen as a means of self-fulfillment and contribution to society, may undergo a radical transformation. While some professions become automated, others may emerge, creating new and unexpected opportunities. However, there is a risk that this change occurs at the expense of personal identity and a sense of belonging, as many people will face uncertainty and unemployment. We then ask ourselves: how can we define our value in a world where traditional work is diminished and human contribution is called into question?

The challenge is not just economic; it is deeply social and cultural. How are our daily interactions influenced by the presence of AI? Virtual assistants, social robots, and algorithm-driven social media platforms are changing the way we communicate and relate to one another. Our friendships, the way we connect with others, and even our concept of community are being questioned. If our interactions are mediated by technology, how can we keep our humanity authentic? The issue becomes increasingly urgent as we immerse ourselves in an era where human contact can be replaced by interactions with artificial entities.

Moreover, AI raises important ethical and moral questions. If machines can make complex decisions, who is responsible for their actions? In a world where decisions are increasingly delegated to automated systems, it is essential to question how these choices influence our daily lives and the values we uphold. Delegating responsibility to a machine raises questions about individual autonomy and the ability to influence our destiny. Are we ready to let machines decide for us? And, if so, at what cost?

The change that AI brings goes far beyond the practical aspects of work tasks or daily interactions; it requires deep reflection on our essence as human beings. Technology, in its advancement, must not only be seen as a tool that improves our lives but also as a phenomenon that changes the rules of the game and challenges our fundamental beliefs. The question it poses is not only "How can we adapt to AI?" but also "How can we ensure that AI serves to enhance humanity rather than dilute its essence?"

In this context, it is vital to engage in an open and inclusive dialogue about what it means to be human in an increasingly automated world. Philosophers, technologists, educators, and citizens must come together to reflect on shared values and aspirations for the future. The choices we make today regarding the development and application of AI will have profound implications for our future.

Economic Regulation and the Role of AI

The question of how to regulate earnings linked to AI is another important aspect of this transformative wave. In an increasingly digital economy, the need for effective regulations becomes evident. The creation of a regulatory framework capable of addressing the complexities of AI is crucial for ensuring that technological innovation does not undermine the well-being of society as a whole. The regulatory landscape must evolve to safeguard individual rights and promote fairness in an economic system increasingly influenced by algorithms.

To regulate earnings linked to AI, it is necessary to consider various factors. First, transparency is essential. The mechanisms behind algorithms must be understood and analyzed to prevent discrimination or bias. When an AI system makes a decision, such as hiring or granting loans, it is essential to ensure that the process is fair and just. To achieve this, regulators should promote clear guidelines on data usage, requiring companies to disclose how data is collected, processed, and used to make decisions. A system of accountability must be established, allowing for independent assessments of algorithms to ensure that they operate ethically and do not discriminate against marginalized groups.

Second, a fair distribution of the economic benefits generated by AI is necessary. The wealth created by automation and intelligent technologies should not be concentrated in the hands of a few but should contribute to social well-being. This requires policies aimed at redistributing wealth, such as progressive taxation on companies that heavily rely on AI. The revenue generated could then be reinvested in social programs, education, and technological training for workers affected by automation. By promoting a fairer distribution of resources, society can ensure that AI becomes an ally in the fight against inequality rather than exacerbating existing disparities.

Furthermore, investments in education and retraining are fundamental to equipping workers with the skills needed to thrive in an AI-driven economy. Governments, companies, and educational institutions must collaborate to develop training programs that prepare individuals for new roles emerging in a technology-driven world. Providing access to high-quality education and ongoing training opportunities is essential to ensure that the workforce is capable of adapting to the changes brought about by AI.

In addition, international cooperation is vital to address the global nature of AI. The development and deployment of AI technologies are not limited to national borders; therefore, cooperation between governments is essential to establish common standards and norms. Initiatives for international collaboration could promote ethical AI practices and ensure that the benefits of technology are accessible to all, regardless of geographical location.

In conclusion, the economic regulation of earnings linked to AI is a multifaceted challenge that requires the joint effort of various stakeholders. Transparency, fairness, and education are key components to create a future where AI serves as a tool for the collective benefit of society. By implementing effective regulations and promoting equitable policies, we can ensure that technological innovation enhances the well-being of humanity, rather than deepening divisions and inequalities.

The Future: Regulation and Technological Innovation

As we look to the future, it becomes increasingly clear that the relationship between regulation and technological innovation must be based on collaboration rather than conflict. Governments and companies must work together to create a regulatory environment that supports innovation while protecting society from potential risks. Regulation should not be seen as a barrier to progress but as a means to promote responsible and sustainable development.

One way to foster this collaboration is through public-private partnerships aimed at exploring innovative solutions to societal challenges. For example, collaboration between technology companies and public institutions could lead to the development of AI solutions capable of addressing pressing issues, such as climate change, health care, and education. By working together, stakeholders can harness the potential of AI to create positive and lasting impacts on society.

Moreover, creating a culture of ethics within technology companies is crucial for ensuring that AI development prioritizes social responsibility. Ethical guidelines should be integrated into every phase of the innovation process, from research and development to implementation. Companies should be encouraged to invest in impact assessments that evaluate the potential social consequences of their technologies.

By adopting an ethical approach to innovation, organizations can ensure that their products contribute positively to society and do not exacerbate existing inequalities or risks.

Finally, fostering a culture of innovation among individuals is vital. Citizens should be encouraged to engage actively with technology, exploring its potential and expressing their concerns about its impact on society. Initiatives that promote digital literacy and critical thinking can empower individuals to navigate an increasingly complex technological landscape and advocate for responsible and ethical use of AI.

We are on the threshold of a new era in which artificial intelligence profoundly transforms our lives and societies. The choices we make today will shape the future we envision and the values we uphold. It is essential to embrace this change with an open mind and heart, recognizing the potential of AI to enhance our lives while remaining vigilant about the ethical, social, and economic implications it entails.

As we prepare for a future where AI plays a central role, we must remember that technology should serve humanity, not the other way around. By promoting responsible development, ethical regulations, and education, we can ensure that AI becomes a force for good in our world. The challenge is great, but so is the opportunity. Together, we can shape a future in which AI enhances our lives, empowers our communities, and drives progress toward a more just and equitable society.

8.1.2 Work and the Disappearance of Historical Professions

The first challenge related to artificial intelligence and job automation is a matter of great importance. Professions that were once deemed irreplaceable, such as those in manufacturing, customer service, and services, are rapidly disappearing as AI and automated technologies take over tasks that, until recently, required a human touch. In many industries, robots and intelligent systems have become capable of performing complex operations with precision and efficiency that surpass human capabilities. This phenomenon has raised legitimate concerns about technological unemployment, a tangible threat to millions of workers.

The impact of this transformation is not uniform. Those in lower positions, particularly in manufacturing and service sectors, are the most vulnerable to automation. Many of these workers are engaged in repetitive and standardized tasks that are easy to replace with automated systems. However, even traditionally considered "cognitive" professions, such as accounting and consulting, are undergoing significant transformation. AI can process and analyze vast amounts of data in record time, reducing the need for human staff in roles that previously required analytical and decision-making skills. This shift highlights an alarming reality: the idea that human work is secure and protected is being reevaluated.

Individuals who cannot retrain for more technologically advanced occupations risk being excluded from an economy that rewards technical knowledge and the ability to collaborate with machines. This leads to another dimension of the challenge: social inequality. Those with the right skills to exploit the opportunities created by AI, such as data science experts, software engineers, and automation specialists, will thrive, while those who fall behind risk being marginalized. The income gap between these two groups could widen significantly, creating an increasingly marked economic and social divide.

This situation raises fundamental questions about the sustainability of modern society and the role of education. If the future of work requires a continuous evolution of skills, it is essential to reflect on how educational systems can adapt to meet the new market demands. In an era where technological innovation advances at a frantic pace, educational institutions must embrace a more flexible and dynamic approach that prepares individuals not only for today's professions but also for those of tomorrow.

Moreover, education should not be limited to providing technical skills; it should also cultivate soft skills such as critical thinking, creativity, and teamwork. These skills will be crucial for effectively interacting with emerging technologies and solving complex problems in an increasingly automated work environment. Adaptability thus becomes a crucial quality for the future workforce, and educational policies must reflect this necessity.

The issue of inclusivity is equally central. How can we ensure that learning and retraining opportunities are accessible to everyone, regardless of their socio-economic background? The current educational system in many parts of the world presents significant barriers for individuals from disadvantaged backgrounds. Investing in vocational training programs, distance learning initiatives, and reskilling support can help mitigate the risk of exclusion. It is imperative to develop innovative solutions to engage those most at risk, ensuring that no one is left behind.

Finally, it is important to consider the psychological impact of this transition. Job loss and uncertainty about the future can have devastating effects on individuals' mental well-being. People may experience anxiety, stress, and a sense of helplessness in the face of a change that seems beyond their control. Therefore, it is essential that policies and initiatives addressing technological unemployment not only focus on training but also on psychological support and career counseling.

8.2 Humanity in the Age of AI

It is not just work that is being questioned. The way we conceive ourselves as human beings is also changing. AI poses challenges to the concepts of creativity, moral decision-making, and even emotion. Machines are learning to generate art, write texts, and compose music. Although these results are still far from emulating human experience in its entirety, we are faced with a philosophical question: if a machine can do what we do, and sometimes do it better, what truly makes us unique?

In a world where AI makes decisions on our behalf—be it in financial investments, medical diagnoses, or advice on interpersonal relationships—there is a risk of losing control over our destiny. Delegating choices to technology could lead to a sense of alienation and helplessness. This phenomenon raises crucial ethical questions about how we want to manage the relationship between humans and machines.

8.2.1 Creativity, Emotion, and Human Identity in the Age of AI

One of the most intriguing questions in the age of artificial intelligence concerns the nature of creativity and emotions. For centuries, humanity has considered creativity a distinctive trait of being human, tied to the ability to interpret the world through art, music, writing, and imagination. However, with the development of advanced AI algorithms capable of generating works of art, literary texts, and music, our understanding of what is truly "creative" is changing.

Today, algorithms such as those used by OpenAI, DeepMind, and others are capable of producing works that imitate human artistic styles, composing poetry, creating paintings, and even writing novels. Although these results are often the fruit of complex processing based on vast amounts of pre-existing data, we cannot ignore that such productions can compete with human works, to the extent that it is often not immediately apparent the difference between a human artist's work and that of an artificial intelligence. For example, in visual art, tools like DALL•E or MidJourney have demonstrated that AI can create stunning images from simple textual descriptions. Similarly, AI-based music creators have shown they can compose evocative melodies that can elicit strong emotions.

This capability of machines raises deep philosophical and ontological questions: if a machine can generate art, write stories, or compose music that can touch the human soul, can we still consider creativity an exclusively human trait? Some philosophers and theorists argue that human creativity is driven by personal experiences, emotions, and intentionality—elements completely absent in artificial intelligence, which lacks consciousness, self-awareness, or intentions of its own. The works created by AI, therefore, may be perceived as simulations rather than authentic expressions.

Nonetheless, the issue becomes increasingly nuanced. If art is evaluated solely based on its ability to evoke emotion or aesthetic reaction, then AI's products can fully qualify as works of art. However, if art is understood as a means of expressing human experience, and the intentionality behind the work is considered fundamental, then a strong boundary remains between human and artificial creativity.

The concept of emotion, another cornerstone of human identity, is also under scrutiny from AI. Today's chatbots and virtual assistants, equipped with advanced language models, can simulate empathy and understand emotional context, adapting to users' responses. While they are algorithms devoid of consciousness and real feelings, they can manipulate human emotions. This has led to ethical debates about how much we should allow machines to interact emotionally with individuals, especially considering that such interactions can lead people to perceive machines as having their own humanity, creating an illusory emotional bond.

Creativity and emotions have always been integral parts of what defines us as human beings. In this sense, artificial intelligence seems to challenge these concepts. However, rather than robbing us of our essence, it forces us to redefine what it truly means to be human in an increasingly technological world. The confrontation with AI could push us to reflect more deeply on our identity, making us more aware of the intrinsic value of human experiences and emotions.

8.2.2 Delegating Decisions and the Risk of Alienation: Where Does Human Control Stop?

Another critical aspect of the interaction between humans and AI is the growing trend of delegating complex decisions to machines that once required human judgment. Artificial intelligence algorithms are already used to make decisions in crucial sectors such as finance, healthcare, and even personal relationships, raising doubts about the impact of this delegation on human autonomy and control over their own destiny.

In the financial world, for example, many investment decisions are now entrusted to automated AI-based systems, such as robo-advisors, which analyze vast amounts of data and apply predictive models to decide where to invest users' money. In theory, such systems can optimize returns and reduce risks, but they raise concerns about how much people can truly understand and monitor the decisions made by machines on their behalf. Investors may feel alienated or distanced from the decision-making processes, blindly trusting machines without fully understanding the risks or consequences of the choices made.

A field where the delegation of decisions to AI is even more controversial is healthcare. Today, AI algorithms are used to assist doctors in diagnosing diseases, planning treatments, and even in robotic surgery. While AI can contribute to greater accuracy and speed in diagnoses, it can also lead to an excessive dependence on technology, reducing the autonomy of medical professionals and, potentially, the trust of patients in their doctors. The ethical question becomes: who has the final say? If artificial intelligence makes a wrong decision, who is responsible for it? Relying too much on AI can undermine human control over fundamental processes that require a holistic, empathetic, and personalized approach—characteristics that machines do not possess.

Another example is the influence of AI on interpersonal relationships. Social media algorithms, designed to maximize user engagement, can significantly influence interactions and personal opinions. The personalization of content, based on users' tastes and habits, creates information bubbles that can alter how people view the world, reducing their exposure to diverse viewpoints. This can generate a kind of cognitive alienation, where people stop making decisions based on personal reflections, instead delegating them to algorithms that suggest friendships, political opinions, and even romantic relationships.

These examples highlight an increasing risk: the more we delegate decisions to artificial intelligence, the more we risk losing touch with our autonomy and ability to choose consciously. This process of delegation can lead to a sense of helplessness, in which individuals feel distanced from the control of their own lives, alienated in a system where machines make decisions for them. Technology, which was supposed to simplify human life, risks paradoxically eroding the sense of personal responsibility and the ability to make informed decisions.

Addressing these risks requires deep reflection on the relationship between humans and machines. We must establish clear limits on how much power we want to delegate to AI, especially in areas that directly affect our lives, our health, and our emotions. Instead of adopting a passive attitude towards technology, we need to cultivate a culture of informed and responsible use of artificial intelligence, where humans retain control over decisions that shape their future.

8.3. The Tax Regulation of AI Earnings

Another fundamental aspect of the future of AI concerns the tax regulation of earnings generated through its use. AI has become a significant source of income for companies and individuals, but the taxation of such earnings remains a gray area in many countries. Many of the earnings produced by AI are digital, intangible, and often distributed globally, making it complex to precisely define where and how they should be taxed.

8.3.1. The Dilemma of International Taxation of AI

One of the main challenges in the tax regulation of AI is its transnational nature. Companies that use AI to generate profits may operate in one country but have servers, algorithms, and users in another. This creates a "tax nexus" problem, which involves identifying where economic activity occurs and, consequently, where the profits should be taxed. The taxation of digital enterprises is already at the center of intense international debate, but with the advent of AI, the problem becomes even more complex.

Currently, existing regulatory frameworks, such as the OECD's proposal for a Global Minimum Tax, attempt to address the issue of digital earnings from large multinationals, but there is still much to be done to comprehensively regulate the field of artificial intelligence. Governments must find a balance between promoting technological innovation and ensuring that companies pay their fair share of taxes on earnings derived from the use of AI.

8.3.2. The Risk of Tax Evasion

The rapid expansion of artificial intelligence (AI) in the global economic landscape has raised significant questions regarding its tax regulation. One of the most serious risks associated with this evolution is the increasing possibility of tax evasion, which undermines the sustainability of local and national economies. The lack of a clear and coherent framework for taxing AI has created a regulatory vacuum that companies, particularly large ones, can exploit to their advantage.

Large technology companies developing AI algorithms, such as Silicon Valley giants, have demonstrated a remarkable ability to maneuver their corporate structures to optimize profits and reduce tax burdens. One of the most common techniques used in this context is the transfer of intellectual property rights. These companies frequently move patent rights and licenses to countries with favorable tax regimes, taking advantage of more permissive tax regulations to declare their profits. As a result, tax revenues in the countries where economic activity actually takes place suffer a negative impact. This phenomenon not only reduces state tax revenues but also places greater pressure on citizens and small and medium-sized enterprises that cannot enjoy the same tax advantages.

Moreover, the global context makes it difficult to monitor and regulate these evasive practices. Companies can easily transfer their profits through complex networks of subsidiaries and offshore companies, further complicating tax authorities' efforts to recover owed revenues. This ever-evolving regulatory landscape has led to a situation where larger, wealthier companies can navigate legal loopholes, while small entrepreneurs and fixed-income workers face an increasingly burdensome tax system.

The issue of tax evasion related to AI is not just an economic matter but also has profound ethical and social implications. When companies do not contribute fairly to the public budget, a disparity arises in investment opportunities for public services, education, healthcare, and infrastructure. This gap amplifies economic and social inequality, generating discontent among citizens who feel neglected by a system that seems to reward only the powerful.

To effectively address this issue, an internationally coordinated approach is necessary. Cooperation among nations is essential to develop common tax standards that can combat tax evasion and ensure that profits are taxed where they are actually generated. This requires not only a review of existing tax regulations but also the implementation of transparency measures that compel companies to clearly and honestly declare their economic activities.

Furthermore, international tax structures must be rethought to reflect the new economic realities created by digitalization and automation. Innovative tax models, such as taxing digital activities, could represent a solution to the challenges related to tax evasion. These models could include applying taxes on revenues generated from digital activities, regardless of the legal domicile of the company, thus ensuring that even companies operating virtually contribute fairly to the tax revenue of the nations in which they operate.

The discussion on how to tackle the risk of tax evasion related to AI is therefore a crucial issue that requires ongoing attention from governments, institutions, and citizens. The need for a clear and robust regulatory framework is evident, as is the demand for a collective commitment to ensure that the opportunities created by artificial intelligence are shared equitably and do not concentrate wealth in the hands of a few.

Chapter 9

The Legal Approach to AI: An Incomplete Framework

On the regulatory front, AI represents an immense challenge for lawmakers. While technological advancements are progressing at an accelerated pace, laws are often slow to adapt. Currently, many countries are just beginning to explore how to regulate AI in a way that can be harnessed for the common good without jeopardizing the rights of citizens or economic and social security.

9.1. AI Regulation: An Evolving Framework

The most advanced regulatory initiatives concern the regulation of responsibilities related to the use of AI. In Europe, the European Commission has proposed an "AI Regulation" aimed at establishing clear standards for the use of artificial intelligence, especially in high-risk sectors such as healthcare and finance. This regulation establishes strict rules to ensure that AI is used transparently, fairly, and safely, with rigorous oversight measures to prevent abuses or discrimination.

However, the regulatory landscape remains fragmented and incomplete. Many countries lack specific laws addressing issues such as the unlawful use of AI, privacy violations, or the attribution of liability in cases of errors generated by autonomous systems. This regulatory void can create legal uncertainties that could hinder the safe and responsible adoption of technology.

9.1.1. Ethical and Legal Dilemmas

In addition to formal regulation, AI raises ethical dilemmas that require deep reflection. As a society, we must decide which types of AI are acceptable and how to balance technological benefits with the protection of individual rights. Some countries have begun to explore the possibility of creating a legal framework to establish the rights and duties of intelligent machines, but there is still a long way to go.

Another crucial theme is the issue of legal liability in the event of damage caused by AI. If an artificial intelligence algorithm makes an erroneous decision, who is responsible? The software producer, the company using it, or the machine itself? The legal framework will need to evolve to address these fundamental questions.

9.1.2. A Future to Govern Wisely

Artificial intelligence represents one of the greatest technological revolutions of our time, bringing with it unprecedented opportunities, but also complex risks and challenges that cannot be overlooked. Like all disruptive innovations, AI has the potential to profoundly transform our way of living, working, and interacting, but its impact will entirely depend on how we choose to manage it as a society. In this sense, it is essential to adopt a reflective and responsible approach that considers not only the immediate benefits but also the long-term consequences.

One of the main risks associated with the large-scale adoption of artificial intelligence is the increasing human alienation. With the automation of many tasks, both intellectual and manual, people may feel increasingly distant from the activities that once constituted the core of their sense of identity and purpose. Tasks that give meaning to daily life, such as creative work, solving complex problems, and decision-making, could be partially or completely replaced by machines, leading to an existential crisis for many individuals. Technologies that replace human work may push us to reconsider our very definition of achievement and utility, with profound cultural and psychological impacts. For this reason, it is necessary to develop a collective dialogue that explores how we can maintain control over our lives and choices without becoming mere spectators of technological progress.

The impact of AI on economic inequality is equally significant. The concentration of technological power in the hands of a few large companies could further widen the gap between the rich and the poor, both nationally and globally. Nations and businesses that can develop and implement AI more rapidly may reap significant economic benefits, leaving behind those that lack the necessary resources or expertise. This scenario could lead to new forms of technological colonialism, where advanced countries or sectors dominate the global market through exclusive access to cutting-edge technologies, while other nations or communities remain trapped in economic and technological dependence. At the individual level, unskilled workers or those with obsolete skills may be the most affected, at risk of being excluded from the job market in the absence of adequate retraining programs and economic support.

The issue of tax evasion, a problem already significant in the digital economy, is further accentuated by the introduction of artificial intelligence. Companies using AI to generate profits may exploit current regulatory gaps to avoid paying taxes fairly, increasing the tax burden on citizens and small businesses. In a context where financial operations are becoming increasingly complex and automated, the ability of governments to adequately monitor and tax economic activities is at risk. To address this challenge, new regulatory tools will be necessary to ensure that technology companies contribute fairly to the well-being of the societies in which they operate, promoting a more equitable redistribution of resources.

However, regulatory uncertainty remains one of the greatest obstacles in the process of regulating AI. Current laws are not sufficiently updated to address the new ethical and legal questions raised by the use of artificial intelligence. The speed at which AI-related technologies are developing far outpaces the ability of governments and institutions to adapt regulatory frameworks. This creates a gray area where technologies advance without being adequately regulated, leaving room for abuses and potential harm to society. For example, automated decisions made by AI algorithms in sectors such as justice, healthcare, and finance can have a profound impact on people's lives, but often lack the necessary legal structures to ensure transparency, fairness, and accountability.

International cooperation will be essential to tackle these challenges. Artificial intelligence knows no national borders, and its development and implementation cannot be confined to a single jurisdiction. It is therefore crucial for governments around the world to collaborate to create global standards that can govern the use of AI ethically and safely. In this context, international organizations such as the United Nations and the European Union can play a key role in defining common guidelines that ensure the benefits of artificial intelligence are shared equitably and its negative implications minimized.

Governing AI will require wisdom and foresight. Governments, businesses, and civil society must work together to define an ethical and regulatory framework that balances technological innovation with the protection of human rights and collective well-being. A fundamental element of this approach will be to ensure that AI is used to enhance the quality of life for people, without sacrificing human dignity and individual autonomy. This implies not only establishing clear rules but also promoting widespread digital literacy, enabling people to understand and actively participate in decision-making processes concerning AI.

In the economic context, it will be essential to ensure that the gains generated by artificial intelligence are distributed fairly. This can be achieved through fiscal policies that encourage wealth redistribution and investments in sectors such as education and vocational training, ensuring that all segments of the population have access to the opportunities created by AI. The challenge is to build an inclusive economy where AI does not become a further tool of polarization but a driver of progress that can sustain global economic growth and improve living conditions for all.

Therefore, artificial intelligence is not just a revolutionary technology but a test of our ability to wisely govern the transformations that will shape the future. It reflects our collective willingness to address ethical, economic, and social challenges with responsibility and long-term vision. Managing this revolution wisely will not only determine the direction of technological development but also define the core values upon which our societies will rely for decades to come.

Conclusions

As we approach a future shaped by artificial intelligence, it is essential to embrace the opportunities it offers and confront the ethical and practical challenges that arise. Every reader has the chance to become an architect of a tomorrow in which AI is not just a tool but an ally in promoting well-being, justice, and equity.

The real question is how to ensure that change occurs positively and responsibly. It is a fundamental choice: to embrace technology as a vehicle for growth or to allow it to distance us from the essential values of our society. The responsibility for this future is in our hands. The decisions we make today should reflect a vision of harmony between technology and humanity.

Now is the time for deep reflection and determined action, building a future that not only harnesses the potential of artificial intelligence but embodies the values and aspirations of a just and prosperous society. Let us choose a future where artificial intelligence serves humanity and not the other way around.

Dear readers,

I wish to express my sincere gratitude for taking the time to read these pages. Your curiosity and interest are the driving force behind my passion for writing and sharing ideas. Every word has been crafted to stimulate reflection and inspire new approaches to a constantly evolving future.

I hope this journey into the world of artificial intelligence and its potentials has provided you with useful and thought-provoking insights. May you carry with you not only information but also new perspectives and visions for your path ahead.

Thank you for being a part of this adventure.

Sincerely,
Willy Whites

www.ingramcontent.com/pod-product-compliance
Lightning Source LLC
Chambersburg PA
CBHW070356230526
45471CB00006B/2598